Jackie Robinson

Breaking the Color Barrier

By Alan Trussell-Cullen

Published in the United States of America
by the Hameray Publishing Group, Inc.

Text © Alan Trussell-Cullen
Maps © Hameray Publishing Group, Inc.
Published 2009

Publisher: Raymond Yuen
Series Editors: Adria F. Klein and Alan Trussell-Cullen
Project Editor: Kaitlyn Nichols
Designers: Lois Stanfield and Amy Stirnkorb
Map Designer: Barry Age

Photo Credits: AP: pages 10, 31, 33
Corbis: front cover, pages 1, 13, 21, 23, 25, 26–27, 28
Getty: back cover, pages 4, 15, 18

All rights reserved. No part of this publication may be reproduced
or transmitted in any form or by any means without permission in
writing from the publisher. Reproduction of any part of this book,
through photocopy, recording, or any electronic or mechanical
retrieval system without the written permission of the publisher,
is an infringement of the copyright law.

ISBN 978-1-60559-063-9

Printed in China

1 2 3 4 5 SIP 13 12 11 10 09

Contents

Chapter 1	**Changing Baseball Forever**	5
Chapter 2	**Athlete in the Making**	7
Chapter 3	**Fighting for Civil Rights in the Army**	14
Chapter 4	**Fighting for Civil Rights in Baseball**	17
Chapter 5	**Jackie Robinson: Baseball Sensation**	24
Chapter 6	**Jackie Robinson: Number 42**	30
Timeline		34
Glossary		36
Learn More		38
Index		39

Chapter 1

Changing Baseball Forever

On April 15, 1947, the Brooklyn Dodgers came out onto the field for a game that would make baseball history. On the team that day was the first African-American to play **Major League Baseball**. His name was Jackie Robinson.

Jackie Robinson knew that many people in the crowd would shout **racist insults** at him. He knew that many of the players didn't think a black man belonged in baseball. But he also knew he had earned the right to be there. He was going to play so well they would have to accept him.

◀ Jackie Robinson was the first African-American to play in Major League Baseball.

For over fifty years, Major League Baseball had been a sport for whites only. There was an unwritten rule that had kept African-American players out of Major League Baseball because of the color of their skin. The rule was called "the color line."

It was a barrier Jackie Robinson was determined to break. He wasn't going to just help win the game for his team that day. He was going to win it for **civil rights** and for his country, too. This is the story of how one man helped break the color barrier in sports forever.

> *"There's not an American in this country free until every one of us is free."*
> —Jackie Robinson

Chapter 2
Athlete in the Making

Jackie was born in Cairo, Georgia in 1919. He was the youngest of five children.

When he was a year old, his father left the family. His mother took the family to Pasadena, California. It was hard raising a family as a single mom. It was also hard being African-American at this time in the United States. African-Americans couldn't sit with white people on buses or even eat at the same restaurants. They had to put up with people calling them racist names. Many years would pass until new laws were made changing the rights for African-Americans and other people of color.

Jackie thought that separating people because of their race was wrong. He didn't think he should be treated differently just because he was black.

> "The right of every American to first-class citizenship is the most important issue of our time."
> —Jackie Robinson

One day when he was eight, a white girl from his street started calling him names. He called her a name back. The girl's father came out of the house and threw a stone at Jackie. Jackie threw one back. Soon both the man and the boy were throwing stones at each other. It only stopped when the man's wife came out and made him stop.

Jackie knew he shouldn't have thrown anything. But he also knew he wanted to stand up for himself.

> *"I'm not concerned with your liking or disliking me . . . All I ask is that you respect me as a human being."* —Jackie Robinson

◀ A police chief stands beside a sign for a whites-only waiting room at a bus terminal.

In high school, Jackie was already starting to shine as an all-around athlete. He played baseball, football, basketball, and tennis. His skills at the broad jump and as a runner made him a track and field star at his school.

Jackie went on to college at the University of California, Los Angeles. At UCLA he was the first athlete to win **varsity letters** in four sports: baseball, basketball, football, and track. He had almost finished his studies at college but had to leave because he was running out of money.

▲ Jackie Robinson was a standout football player at UCLA.

Chapter 3

Fighting for Civil Rights in the Army

In 1941 the Japanese bombed the naval base at Pearl Harbor in Hawaii. America was now fighting in World War II. Robinson **enlisted** in the U.S. Army. But even in the army Robinson would find **racism**.

One night, while training in Texas, Robinson was going home on a bus. He took his seat. Suddenly, the bus driver started shouting at him. He told Robinson he was sitting in a seat meant only for white people and he had to move to the back of the bus. Robinson refused to move. This landed him

Jackie Robinson was a second lieutenant in the army. ▶

in a lot of trouble with the army. But he stood up for his rights and eventually he was let go without a fine or time in jail.

Robinson knew that it wasn't right that people were **segregated**, or kept apart, because of their race. But African-Americans weren't just kept out of bus seats, restaurants, schools, and neighborhoods because of their race. They were also kept out of major league sports. This would be Robinson's next big struggle.

Chapter 4

Fighting for Civil Rights in Baseball

In the 1940's Major League Baseball players were all white. African-American players had to play in the Negro Baseball League. The segregation of "the color line" had been happening in baseball for over fifty years.

But one man wanted to change this. He was Branch Rickey, the manager of the Brooklyn Dodgers. He wanted the best players for his team, regardless of race. He had a secret plan. He wanted to find a black player who would help his team to win. But he also had to find a player who had the courage to stay calm—even if people were shouting insults and calling him names.

▲ Branch Rickey and Jackie Robinson in 1949.

He sent scouts all over the country to find that player.

At the time, Jackie Robinson was playing for the Kansas City Monarchs in the Negro Baseball League. One day a scout tapped Robinson on the shoulder.

"Branch Rickey wants to meet you," he said.

Rickey told Robinson he wanted him to play for the all-white Brooklyn Dodgers. He said it would be hard being the only black man out there on the field. But he told Robinson to stay calm and not fight back, no matter what people shouted or did.

"Mr. Rickey," Robinson asked, "are you looking for someone who is afraid to fight back?"

"Robinson," said Mr. Rickey, "I'm looking for a ballplayer with guts enough *not* to fight back!"

Jackie Robinson promised to stay calm and see what happened for just one year.

His first game for the Dodgers was on April 15, 1947. The night before, Jackie Robinson was very nervous. He didn't know what the white baseball fans would do or say.

But when Robinson got out on the field, he felt good. There were only a few boos from the fans. He played well.

It was a big day for him, but it was an even bigger day for baseball. At last someone had broken the fifty-year-old color barrier.

Soon after, the Dodgers played a big game against Jersey City. The Dodgers were playing well. By the second inning, Jersey City still hadn't been able to score any runs. Then it was the Dodgers turn to bat.

Halfway through the inning, the Dodgers had two men on base. Jackie Robinson came up to bat. He swung. It was a huge hit! The ball flew 340 feet over the left field fence! He had hit his first home run in Major League Baseball! The crowd went wild!

▲ Jackie Robinson is congratulated by his teammate after hitting his first home run in the major league.

But all games were not like that one. One of the worst games was in Syracuse, New York. The problem wasn't racial insults from the fans in the crowd, but from the team they were playing. They kept calling Jackie racist names. Then halfway through the game, one of their players threw a live black cat out onto the field.

"Hey Jackie," the player shouted, "there's your cousin!"

Robinson answered by scoring the next run. As he passed the other player's dugout he shouted, "I guess my cousin's pretty happy now!"

Some of Jackie Robinson's best support came from other players, like Pee Wee Reese, the Dodgers' team captain.

One day the crowd was very nasty. They were jeering and shouting racist names. Suddenly, Reese came over and put his arm around Robinson. Then he turned to face the crowd. It was as if he were saying,

"This is a great player and I am proud to have him on my team."

The jeering stopped and everyone else began to cheer. Photographs of Jackie Robinson and Pee Wee Reese appeared in newspapers throughout the country.

▲ The Dodgers' infield in the dugout. Pee Wee Reese is second from the left, Jackie Robinson is on the far right.

Chapter 5

Jackie Robinson: Baseball Sensation

In his first year with the Dodgers, Jackie Robinson hit twelve home runs and helped the Dodgers win the National League pennant. He led the National League in stolen bases and was chosen as **Rookie of the Year**.

In the years that followed, Robinson went on to delight fans. They began to flock to his games to watch him play. In 1949 he had an outstanding batting average of .342. He was very good at **stealing bases**, too. In that year he managed to steal more bases than anyone else.

Jackie Robinson signing autographs at spring training. ▶

▲ Jackie Robinson stealing a base and sliding into home plate.

People were now calling him a hero. There was even a popular song about him called "Did You See Jackie Robinson Hit that Ball?" At the time, Robinson was the highest-paid athlete of any race in Dodgers' history.

In 1950 a movie was made about him called *The Jackie Robinson Story*. Though it was unusual, Jackie Robinson played himself in the movie and it was very popular.

Robinson helped his team, the Dodgers, win the National League pennant several times. Finally in 1955, they beat the New York Yankees to win the World Series.

Jackie Robinson's success wasn't just a victory for baseball. It was a victory for civil rights, too. Now other great African-Americans were chosen to play for the big teams.

> *"Life is not a spectator sport. If you're going to spend your whole life in the grandstand just watching what goes on, in my opinion you're wasting your life."*
> —Jackie Robinson

◀ **Jackie Robinson on set at the filming of *The Jackie Robinson Story*.**

Chapter 6

Jackie Robinson: Number 42

In 1957 Jackie Robinson retired from baseball and became a businessman. But he continued to push for equality in sports. In 1962 he was **inducted** into the Baseball Hall of Fame—the first African-American to receive the honor.

In his later life, Jackie Robinson's health began to decline and on October 24, 1972, he died. It was a sad day for baseball and for the country.

Jackie Robinson holds a plaque commemorating his induction into the Baseball Hall of Fame in 1962. ▶

> "He struck a mighty blow for equality, freedom, and the American way of life. Jackie Robinson was a good citizen, a great man, and a true American champion."
>
> —President Ronald Reagan

The years would pass, but Jackie Robinson continued to inspire people and change their lives. On April 15, 1997, baseball players everywhere celebrated the fiftieth anniversary of his historic first Major League Baseball game. His jersey number was 42. As part of the fiftieth anniversary celebrations, his number was officially **retired** from Major League Baseball. From that day on, no major league player would be allowed to wear that number. The number 42 will always be remembered as Jackie Robinson's number.

Jackie Robinson will be remembered, too. He will be remembered as a great player and as a great sportsman. But above all, he will be remembered as a great champion of civil rights. By his skill and courage, he changed sports in America forever.

Timeline

1919 Jackie Robinson is born in Cairo, Georgia, on July 31

1920 Jackie's mother moves the family to Pasadena, California

1935 Attends John Muir High School where he plays five sports: football, basketball, track, baseball, and tennis

1940 Attends the University of California, Los Angeles (UCLA); is the first athlete to win varsity letters in four sports: baseball, basketball, football, and track

1941 Leaves UCLA without graduating because of financial reasons

1941 Japanese bomb Pearl Harbor, December 7; the U.S. enters World War II

1942 Enlists in the U.S. Army

1944 Gets into trouble with the army for refusing to sit in the back of a segregated bus; is later let off without any fines

1945 Is chosen by Branch Rickey to play for the Brooklyn Dodgers

1947 Makes baseball history on April 15 by being the first African-American to play for a major league team in more than fifty years

1947 Wins Rookie of the Year Award

1949 Awarded the title "Most Valuable Player" in the National League with a .342 batting average and thirty-seven stolen bases

1950 Plays himself in a movie made about his life, *The Jackie Robinson Story*

1955 Dodgers beat the New York Yankees to win the 1955 World Series

1957 Retires and goes into business

1962 Is the first African-American inducted into the Baseball Hall of Fame

1972 Dies, October 24

1997 The world celebrates the fiftieth anniversary of Jackie's historic breaking of Major League Baseball's color line; his jersey number 42 is retired

Glossary

Baseball Hall of Fame — a national museum that celebrates the greatest baseball players in history

civil rights — rights guaranteed by the Constitution that all people have to be treated fairly and equally, regardless of their race, religious beliefs, age, or gender

enlisted — joined the military

inducted — officially invited or admitted into an important organization or place

Major League Baseball — the highest level of play in professional baseball

racism — prejudice or discrimination based on a person's race

racist insults — hurtful things said to a person based on their race

retired	when a person finally leaves their work; in sports, a retired player's number means that number is no longer being used
Rookie of the Year	award given in a number of sports to the best first year player
segregated	kept separate or apart
stealing bases	when a baseball player on a base manages to run safely to the next base before the catcher can throw the ball to that base
varsity letter	an award earned in the United States for excellence in a school or college activity or sport. They are usually large cloth letters that can be sewn onto one's clothing.

Learn More

Books

I Never Had It Made: An Autobiography of Jackie Robinson by Jackie Robinson and Alfred Duckett (Harper Perennial, 2003)

Jackie Robinson and the Big Game by Dan Gutman (Aladdin, 2006)

Jackie Robinson Breaks the Color Line by Andrew Santella (Children's Press, 1996)

Jackie Robinson: Strong Inside and Out (Time for Kids) by Time for Kids Editors (HarperCollins, 2005)

Promises to Keep: How Jackie Robinson Changed America by Sharon Robinson (Scholastic, 2004)

Thank You, Jackie Robinson by Barbara Cohen (HarperCollins, 1997)

Websites

www.afroam.org/history/Robinson/intro.html
www.jackierobinson.com
www.time.com/time/time100/heroes/profile/robinson03.html

Index

athlete 12, 28

baseball 5, 12, 17, 20, 29, 30, 32
Baseball Hall of Fame 30, 36
basketball 12
batting average 24
broad jump 12
Brooklyn Dodgers 5, 17, 19, 20, 22, 24, 28, 29

Cairo 7
California 8
captain 22
champion 33
civil rights 6, 29, 33, 36
college 12
color line, the 6, 17

dugout 22

enlisted 14, 36
equality 30

football 12

Georgia 7

Hawaii 14

inducted 30, 36

Japanese 14
jersey 32

Kansas City Monarchs 19

Los Angeles 12

Major League Baseball 5, 6, 17, 20, 32, 36
manager 17

National League pennant 24, 29
Negro Baseball League 17, 19
New York Yankees 29

Pasadena 8
Pearl Harbor 14

race 8, 16, 17, 28
racism 14, 36
racist insults 5, 36
Reese, Pee Wee 22, 23
retired 30, 32, 37
Rickey, Branch 17, 19
Rookie of the Year 24, 37

scouts 19
segregated 16, 37
stealing bases 24, 37

tennis 12
Texas 14
The Jackie Robinson Story 28
track and field 12

University of California 12

varsity letters 12, 37

World War II 14